UNUSUAL LiFe CYCLES OF

FISH

by Jaclyn Jaycox

CAPSTONE PRESS
a capstone imprint

Capstone Captivate is published by Capstone Press, an imprint of Capstone.
1710 Roe Crest Drive
North Mankato, Minnesota 56003
www.capstonepub.com

Library of Congress Cataloging-in-Publication Data
Names: Jaycox, Jaclyn, 1983- author.
Title: Unusual life cycles of fish / Jaclyn Jaycox.
Description: North Mankato, Minnesota : Pebble, an imprint of Capstone,
[2021] | Series: Unusual life cycles | Includes bibliographical references and
index. | Audience: Ages 8-11 | Audience: Grades 4-6 | Summary: "Have you
ever heard of a male fish that carries eggs? What about a fish that gives
birth to live young? Young readers will learn about seahorses, guppies, and
other fish with unusual life cycles"-- Provided by publisher.
Identifiers: LCCN 2021002823 (print) | LCCN 2021002824 (ebook) | ISBN
9781496695581 (hardcover) | ISBN 9781496697028 (paperback) | ISBN
9781977155238 (pdf) | ISBN 9781977156853 (kindle edition)
Subjects: LCSH: Fishes--Life cycles--Juvenile literature. | Fishes--
Miscellanea--Juvenile literature. Classification: LCC QL617.2 .J39 2021
(print) | LCC QL617.2 (ebook) | DDC 597.156--dc23
LC record available at https://lccn.loc.gov/2021002823
LC ebook record available at https://lccn.loc.gov/2021002824

Image Credits
Dreamstime/Mirkorosenau, 19; Minden Pictures: Norburt Wu, 29, Tony
Wu/NPL, 27; Shutterstock: ABS Natural History, 9, Designua, 7, Karel
Zahradka, 17, livingpitty, 23, Nantawat Chotsuwan, cover, Photofenik, 21,
Rich Carey, 15, Ronnie Chua, 11, Sekar B, 13, Studio 37, 5, underworld, 25

Design elements: Shutterstock: emEF, Max Krasnov

Editorial Credits
Editor: Gena Chester; Designer: Bobbie Nuytten; Media Researcher: Kelly
Garvin; Production Specialist: Laura Manthe

All internet sites appearing in back matter were available and accurate
when this book was sent to press.

Words in **bold** are in the glossary.

Table of Contents

CHAPTER 1

Fish Life Cycle

There are more than 20,000 different kinds of fish in the world. Like all other living things, fish go through a life cycle. A life cycle is all the different changes a fish goes through from birth to adulthood. From small ponds to huge oceans, there are amazing transformations that happen below the surface.

Fish begin life as eggs. Females usually lay eggs in the water. Males **fertilize** the eggs. Then the eggs are left to survive on their own. Tiny **larvae** hatch from the eggs. They have a head and tail and are often see-through. The larvae have a yolk sac attached to them. This is their food for the first few days of life. They develop their mouths and eyes. Once the yolk sac is gone, the young fish are called fry.

Fry swim next to an adult discus fish.

Fry are ready to start eating on their own. They continue to grow and develop their fins. Their color changes. They begin to look like miniature adults. The fry stage usually lasts less than a year. Then they are known as **juveniles**. When the fish are able to **reproduce**, they have reached adulthood.

This life cycle is what many fish go through. But there are a few that experience life a bit differently. Some fish live very short lives. Others give birth to live young. And some have to travel great distances to lay their eggs. Let's dive in and take a look at fish with unusual life cycles.

FISH LIFE CYCLE

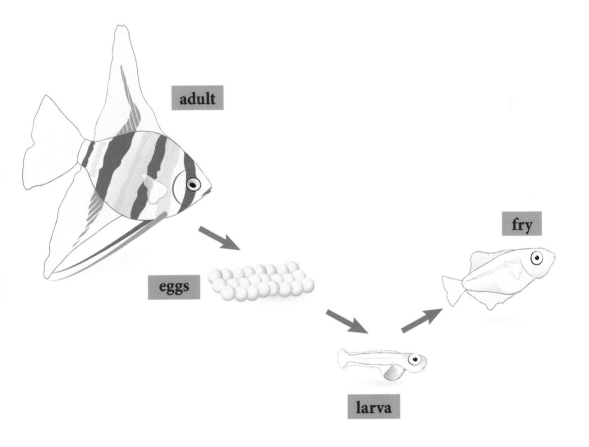

adult

eggs

larva

fry

CHAPTER 2

Long Journeys

European Eels

European eels look different from most fish. They have a small set of fins and long bodies like snakes. European eels travel long distances to lay their eggs. Adults live in freshwater rivers. When they are ready to lay eggs, or **spawn**, they head toward the ocean. They travel thousands of miles. When they reach the ocean, they lay millions of eggs. The adults die after spawning.

The eel eggs float in the water. Small, see-through larvae hatch from the eggs. They float in the ocean **currents** for up to three years. When they get to the coast, they transform into their juvenile stage. They continue floating until reaching the river they will live in. European eels spend up to 20 years in the river before returning to the ocean to lay eggs.

A European eel in River Culm, England

Salmon

A salmon's journey is opposite of an eel's journey. Salmon begin their lives in freshwater rivers. The eggs are hidden under rocks. The **embryos** develop over the winter months. When spring comes, they hatch. They live off their yolk sac for the first few weeks. They stay hidden. When they have grown into fry, they come out from the rocks to start feeding.

Some salmon spend up to two years in rivers before starting their journey to the ocean. Others leave right away. Salmon go through a stage of life called **smolting**. Their gills and kidneys change so they can live in salt water. They start to grow silver scales. They eat a lot on their way to the ocean. It helps them to survive once they get there.

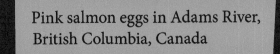

Pink salmon eggs in Adams River,
British Columbia, Canada

Salmon stay near the mouth of the river while their bodies adjust to the salt water. Then they go farther into the ocean to live most of their lives. After about two to six years, adult salmon will be ready to spawn. They begin their journey back to where they were born.

Salmon again spend time at the mouth of the river. They adjust to going back into fresh water. When they reach the area where they were born, the females begin digging. They use their tails to dig holes in the rocks. They lay thousands of eggs. Then a male fertilizes the eggs.

SURVIVAL

Many salmon don't survive after their journey to spawn. They have to swim against the river's current. Bears, otters, and eagles try to catch them. Most salmon stop eating during the trip. They use all their energy to make it upriver.

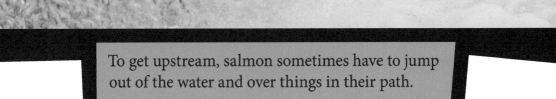

To get upstream, salmon sometimes have to jump out of the water and over things in their path.

CHAPTER 3

Short Life Cycles

Cuttlefish

Unlike most other fish, cuttlefish live short lives. A female lays between 100 and 300 eggs on the ocean floor. She coats the eggs in black ink. It helps to hide them from **predators**. The eggs hatch one to two months later. They hatch as miniature adults. But one is only about the size of a pea. Their eyes are already developed. They start hunting for food right away.

Cuttlefish grow very fast. They reach adulthood after about 18 months. Some grow to be more than 20 pounds (9 kilograms) in that time. Shortly after mating, the male cuttlefish dies. The female will continue to mate and lay eggs until her eggs are all gone. Then she will also die. These fish live no more than two years.

Fact!

Cuttlefish have an amazing ability to blend into their surroundings. They can change color in an instant. It keeps them hidden from predators.

Cuttlefish are cephalopods. Like squid and octopuses, they have tentacles.

Killifish

Killifish have even shorter lives than cuttlefish. Most live their whole lives in just one year. The African turquoise killifish survives only about four months. It is one of the shortest-lived animals in the world. Many killifish in South America and Africa live in pools and puddles created during the wet season. These pools disappear during the dry season. Most killifish die once the pools disappear.

Fact!

Mangrove killifish can survive out of water for more than two months. They stay moist under leaf piles. They hunt on land for insect larvae and worms.

This type of killifish, called blue lyretail, lives in Nigeria and Cameroon.

Killifish lay eggs when the pools fill. When the pools dry up and the adults die, the embryos are left behind in the mud. But they are able to live through the dry season. The embryos stop developing for periods of time. This delays hatching for weeks or even months. Unlike most other fish, killifish aren't born with a yolk sac. If they were to hatch during the dry season, they wouldn't survive.

Eggs hatch when the rain returns and the pools fill. Killifish grow very quickly and start spawning. Some reach adulthood in just 30 days. They must lay their eggs to repeat the life cycle before the pools dry up again.

Killifish eggs

CHAPTER 4

Strange Births

Cichlids

Cichlids are very protective parents. Females lay eggs. But they don't leave them like most other fish do. Instead, most gather up the eggs in their mouths. Their mouths protect the eggs. Females don't open their mouths during this time. Not even to eat! This helps ensure none of the eggs accidentally float away. It can take the eggs about one month to hatch.

Some cichlids release the larvae after they've hatched. But they stay close. If the mother senses danger, she will signal her young. They will swim back into her mouth until the danger has passed. Other cichlids keep their young in their mouths for longer periods of time. The female will gather food in her mouth for the young to eat. Because of how protected these fish are by their mothers, they have a much higher chance of survival compared to other types of fish.

Fact!

Some cichlids don't carry their eggs in their mouths. But they are still protective. The male and female will both guard the eggs.

The jewel cichlid is a freshwater fish.

Guppies

Guppies completely skip a life cycle stage. There is no larval stage. They give birth to live fry. The babies develop inside the females. About a month after mating, females give birth. On average, they have between 30 and 60 babies. But some have had up to 200.

Guppies are able to swim immediately after being born. They quickly find a place to hide from predators. They are smaller than the tip of a pencil when they are born. Many larger fish try to eat them. About two hours after birth, guppies are ready to start eating. They eat bits of plants and **algae**.

Young guppy

Guppies grow quickly and become juveniles at about 4 weeks old. They don't stay in the juvenile stage long. At about 2 months old, guppies start an extra stage of life called the young stage. They are able to have babies of their own. But they are not yet adults. They are still growing.

When guppies are about 6 months old, they reach the adult stage. They are finished growing. They can have babies until they are about 2 years old. Guppies can live up to five years.

Fact!

Guppies are nicknamed "million fish" because they can produce many babies in a short period of time.

Guppies are popular fish for aquariums.

Seahorses

Seahorses are another type of fish that give birth to live young. But the males are the ones to have babies! They are the only male animals on Earth to do so. Male seahorses have a pouch on their stomachs called a brooding pouch. A female lays her eggs in the pouch.

Once the eggs hatch, the babies develop into fry. Usually, this takes two to four weeks. Then the males give birth to fully formed miniature seahorses. Most kinds of seahorses give birth to between 100 and 200 fry. But some larger kinds can have more than 1,500! The young swim away right after birth, ready for life on their own.

MALE PREGNANCIES

Scientists aren't exactly sure why male seahorses carry the babies. But some believe it's so female seahorses can make more eggs while the males are pregnant. After they give birth, males can get pregnant again immediately. Only five out of every 1,000 baby seahorses survive. The ability to have lots of babies helps their species go on.

A male seahorse giving birth

CHAPTER 5

Together Forever

Anglerfish

Most anglerfish live in the deepest, darkest parts of the ocean. They have a very unique way of reproducing. Females are much larger than males. When the two meet, the male bites the female. He doesn't let go. Over time, their bodies **fuse** together. It can be hard to come across a mate in such a dark place. Permanently fusing ensures eggs will always be fertilized. A female can collect several males throughout her life.

Once fused, the males lose their eyes and fins. They live off the female's blood. In return, they fertilize the female's eggs when she spawns. The eggs float up to the surface to hatch. There is more food there for baby anglerfish to eat. As they grow bigger, they return to the depths of the ocean.

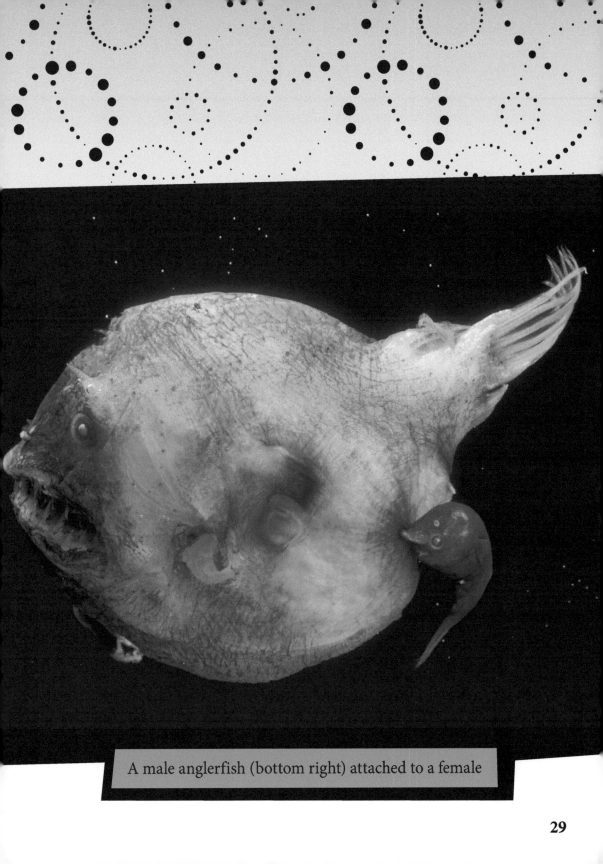

A male anglerfish (bottom right) attached to a female

Glossary

algae (AL-gee)—small plants without roots or stems that grow in water

current (KUHR-uhnt)—the movement of water in a river or an ocean

embryo (EM-bree-oh)—an animal that is just beginning to grow before birth or hatching

fertilize (FUHR-tuh-lyz)—to join an egg of a female with a sperm of a male to produce young

fuse (FYOOZ)—to join together

juvenile (JOO-vuh-nuhl)—young fish

larva (LAR-vuh)—a fish that is not fully developed

predator (PRED-uh-tor)—an animal that hunts other animals for food

reproduce (ree-pruh-DOOSE)—to have offspring

smolt (SMOLT)—a stage of a salmon's life

spawn (SPON)—to lay eggs

Read More

Amstutz, Lisa J. *Investigating Animal Life Cycles*. Minneapolis: Lerner Publications, 2016.

Dickmann, Nancy. *Salmon*. Tucson, AZ: Brown Bear Books, 2020.

Jacobson, Bray. *Fish Life Cycles*. New York: Gareth Stevens Publishing, 2018.

Internet Sites

Easy Science for Kids: Life Cycle of a Fish
https://easyscienceforkids.com/lifecycle-of-a-fish/

Kid Zone: Animal Life Cycles
https://www.kidzone.ws/animals/lifecycle.htm

National Geographic Kids: Seahorse Facts
https://www.natgeokids.com/nz/discover/animals/sea-life/seahorse-facts/

Index